The Interior Plains

Galadriel Watson

Weigl

CALGARY
www.weigl.ca

Published by Weigl Educational Publishers Limited
6325 – 10 Street SE
Calgary, Alberta, Canada
T2H 2Z9

Web site: www.weigl.ca

Library and Archives Canada Cataloguing in Publication

Watson, Galadriel
      The interior plains / Galadriel Watson.
(Canadian geographic regions)
Includes index.
ISBN 1-55388-144-3 (bound).--ISBN 1-55388-151-6 (pbk.)
        1. Northwest Territories--Geography--Textbooks.   2. Prairie
Provinces--Geography--Textbooks.   3. Great Plains--Geography--Textbooks.
I. Title. II. Series.
FC3237.W38 2005   917.12   C2005-904562-0

Printed in United States of America
1 2 3 4 5 6 7 8 9 0   09 08 07 06 05

CREDITS: Every reasonable effort has been made to trace ownership and to obtain permission to
reprint copyright material. The publishers would be pleased to have any errors or omissions brought
to their attention so that they may be corrected in subsequent printings.

COVER: The Interior Plains often consist of expansive and uninterrupted views of the prairie
landscape's wide-open spaces.

Cover: Eastcott Momatiuk/Stone/Getty Images (front); (Darrell Gulin/Stone/Getty Images) (back);
Getty Images: pages 3 (altrendo nature/Altrendo), 4L (Steve Bly/The Image Bank), 4ML (Paul
Nicklen/National Geographic), 4MR (Philip & Karen Smith/Stone), 4R (Francesca York/Dorling
Kindersley), 5L (Raymond K. Gehman/National Geographic), 5M (John Dunn/National Geographic),
5R (Ed Simpson/Stone), 6 (Michael Lewis/National Geographic), 7T (Michael Lewis/National
Geographic), 7B (Philip Schermeister/National Geographic), 11 (Raymond Gehman/National
Geographic), 13 (Hulton Archive), 14 (Todd Korol/Aurora), 15 (Hulton Archive), 16 (Wallace
Kirkland/Time Life Pictures), 17 (Wallace Kirkland/Time Life Pictures), 21 (Raymond
Gehman/National Geographic), 23 (Ross Barnett/Lonely Planet Images), 24 (Corey Wise/Lonely Planet
Images), 25 (Rene Frederick/Photodisc Red), 28 (Three Lions), 29 (Russell Illig/Photodisc Green), 30
(Robert Harding/Digital Vision), 31R (Kenneth Garrett/National Geographic), 32 (George
Hunter/Stone), 33 (Paul Chesley/National Geographic), 34 (altrendo nature/Altrendo), 35 (Theo
Allofs/Photonica), 36 (Darrell Gulin/Stone), 37 (Arthur Morris/Visuals Unlimited), 38 (Photodisc
Collection/Photodisc Blue), 39 (Paul Sisul/Stone), 40 (Raymond Gehman/National Geographic), 41
(Jacques Descloitres/MODIS Land Rapid Response Team at NASA), 42 (Nancy Simmerman/Stone),
43TL (Getty Images/Taxi), 43TR (Nicholas Veasey/Photographer's Choice), 43ML (Tom Schierlitz/The
Image Bank), 43MR (Bill Greenblatt/Liaison), 43BL (Maria Stenzel/National Geographic), 43BR
(Bryce Flynn Photography Inc/Taxi), 44L (Stockdisc/Stockdisc Classic), 44M (Ryan McVay/Photodisc
Green), 44R (C Squared Studios/Photodisc Green), 45L (Tom Schierlitz/The Image Bank), 45R
(Stockdisc/Stockdisc Classic); Roger Paulen/Alberta Geological Survey: page 20; Photos.com: pages
18, 19, 22, 31L.

Copy Editors
Heather Kissock
Frances Purslow
Arlene Worsley

Designer
Terry Paulhus

Layout
Kathryn Livingstone
Gregg Muller

Photo Researchers
Annalise Bekkering
Jennifer Hurtig

We gratefully acknowledge
the financial support of the
Government of Canada through
the Book Publishing Industry
Development Program (BPIDP)
for our publishing activities.

CONTENTS

The Regions of Canada

Canada is the second largest country on Earth. It occupies an enormous area of land on the North American continent. Studying geography helps draw attention to the seven diverse Canadian regions, including their land, climate, vegetation, and wildlife. Learning about geography also helps in understanding the people in each region, their history, and their culture. The word "geography" comes from Greek and means "earth description."

THE APPALACHIAN	THE CANADIAN SHIELD	THE CORDILLERA	THE GREAT LAKES
The Appalachian region is named for the Appalachian mountain range that extends from the United States into eastern Canada. This diverse region contains highlands, lowlands, plateaus, hills, coastal areas, lakes, and rivers.	By far the largest of Canada's geographic regions, the Canadian Shield occupies almost half of the total area of Canada. It is centred around the Hudson Bay. The Canadian Shield is characterized by rocky, poor soil and cold temperatures.	The Cordillera region comprises a series of mountain belts in western Canada. It includes three significant mountain ranges—the Rocky Mountains, Coast Mountains, and Columbia Mountains.	The Great Lakes region is home to five lakes—Lake Superior, Lake Huron, Lake Ontario, Lake Michigan, and Lake Erie. Together, they make up the largest freshwater region in the world.

Canada is home to a variety of landforms. The country hosts sweeping Arctic **tundra**, fertile lowlands, rolling plains, majestic mountains, and vast forests. Each region has a wide range of plants, animals, natural resources, industries, and people.

THE INTERIOR PLAINS	THE NORTH	THE ST. LAWRENCE LOWLANDS
The rolling, low-lying landscape of the Interior Plains is the primary centre for agriculture in Canada. The Interior Plains region lies between the Cordillera and the Canadian Shield.	Much of the North region is composed of thousands of islands north of the Canadian mainland. Distinctive landforms in the region include Arctic lowlands and polar deserts. Glacier mountains are also a recognizable feature in the North.	The St. Lawrence Lowlands region is located on fertile soil surrounding the St. Lawrence River. The region contains a waterway system linking Canada and the United States to the Atlantic Ocean.

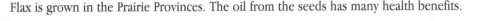

One Divided by Three

The Interior Plains are a region of flat or gently rolling fields that lie in the centre of Canada. **Glaciers** further flattened the land when they crept over it millions of years ago. Any mounds of earth and ground rock they left in their wake are today's **sporadic** hills.

> **"** In total, the Interior Plains account for 18 percent of Canada's land surface, or 1.8 million square kilometres. **"**

The Interior Plains stretch from the Arctic Ocean in the north to the Canada–United States border in the south. On the west, they butt the Rocky Mountain foothills, which mark the edge of the Cordillera. On the east, they lie against the Canadian Shield. The Interior Plains cover nearly all of the province of Alberta, about half of Saskatchewan, and the southwest corner of Manitoba. They extend through the Northwest Territories to the Arctic Ocean. They also take over a small corner of northeastern British Columbia. In total, the Interior Plains account for 18 percent of Canada's land surface, or 1.8 million square kilometres.

Flax is grown in the Prairie Provinces. The oil from the seeds has many health benefits.

Based on elements found on the plains' surface, scientists have divided the Interior Plains into three smaller areas: the prairies, the boreal plains, and the taiga plains.

The Prairies

The prairie area is the reason the provinces of Alberta, Manitoba, and Saskatchewan are called the Prairie Provinces—even though the prairies only cover one third, or less, of each province. The Prairies are known for their fertile farmland, with some of the richest soil in the country.

The Boreal Plains

The boreal plains are part of an area called the boreal forest, or the "spruce-moose biome." The area gets its name from the abundance of spruce trees and moose that live there.

The Taiga Plains

The taiga plains contain a mixture of **coniferous** forests and tundra. These stunted forests are the reason the area earned the name *taiga*, which is Russian for "land of little sticks." This area is home to Canada's longest river, the Mackenzie.

Moose are one of the large herbivores that graze the tall-grass prairie.

QUICK FACTS

- The MacKenzie River is named for explorer Alexander Mackenzie, a Scotsman who mapped and travelled vast areas of western Canada. He was the first European to travel most of the length of this mighty river.

- The early European explorers and settlers had never seen anything like North America's Prairies. There are no prairie regions in Europe that compare to Canada's region, so the French fur traders had no words to describe them. They decided to use *prairie*, the French term for "meadow."

- The word "boreal" comes from the name Boreas. Boreas was the Greek god of the north wind.

Map of Canadian Geographic Regions

This map of Canada shows the seven geographic regions that make up the country. The regions are divided by their topography, from towering mountains to river valleys, and from Arctic tundra to rolling prairies. Canadian geographic regions are some of the most diverse anywhere in the world.

Studying a map of Canada's geographic regions helps develop an understanding of them, and about the nation as a whole.

LEGEND

	The Appalachian
	The Canadian Shield
	The Cordillera
	The Great Lakes
	The Interior Plains
	The North
	The St. Lawrence Lowlands

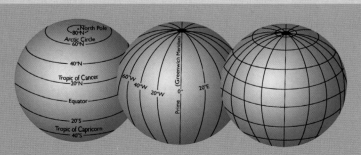

Latitude and Longitude

Longitude measures the distance from a spot on the map to an imaginary line called the prime meridian that runs around the globe from the North Pole to the South Pole.

Latitude measures the distance from a spot on the map to an imaginary line called the equator that runs around the middle of the globe.

The Map Scale

A map scale is a type of formula. The scale helps determine how to calculate distances between places on a map.

```
0          500 Kilometres
```

The Compass Rose

North is indicated on the map by the compass rose. As well, the cardinal directions—north, south, east, and west—and the intermediate directions—northeast, southeast, northwest, southwest—are shown.

Regions of the World

The prairie, boreal, and taiga areas of the Interior Plains are not unique to Canada. Similar areas can be found all over the world. Many scientists believe that the geographic history of Earth and regions around the world share a variety of characteristics.

The Story of Pangaea

The reason Earth has similar regions in different countries is that the world was once made up of one continent that German meteorologist and geologist Alfred Wegener called Pangaea. In 1912, Wegener proposed the theory of continental drift. He theorized that all the land on Earth was part of one large landmass. Pangaea covered nearly half of Earth's surface and was surrounded by an ocean called Panthalassa. Between 245 and 208 million years ago, Pangaea began to split. The pieces of the larger landmass moved apart until they formed seven continents—Africa, Antarctica, Asia, Australia, Europe, North America, and South America.

PERMIAN
225 million years ago

TRIASSIC
200 million years ago

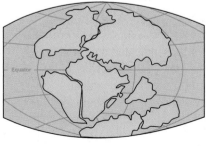

JURASSIC
135 million years ago

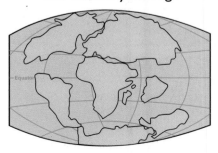

CRETACEOUS
65 million years ago

The Mackenzie River system, which cuts through the taiga plains, is the longest in Canada.

Grassland Prairies

The southern part of the Interior Plains is covered by grassy areas called grasslands. Other grasslands exist around the world. In fact, grasslands can be found on every continent except Antarctica. They cover about 25 percent of all the land on Earth.

In South America, the grasslands are called the Pampas. The Pampas cover about one-fifth of Argentina and are home to more than half of its people. This region has some of the world's best topsoil and is used for farming and ranching.

Another large grassland is the **veld** of South Africa. Similar to the Canadian grasslands, the South African veld is located on a vast area of flat land. It starts at a mountain range, then slopes downward, much like the Interior Plains.

The Boreal Forest

In the northern part of the Interior Plains, the taiga and boreal plains areas include part of the boreal forest. The boreal forest is a vast region that wraps in a band around the world. It sweeps through Canada, over to Norway, Sweden, and Finland, and then on to Russia.

The Taiga

In Russia, the taiga covers most of Siberia and two-fifths of the European part of the country. About one-third of the world's softwood lumber is contained in the Russian taiga.

QUICK FACTS

- If all the grasslands in the world were put together, they would cover about 46 million square kilometres. That is roughly three times the size of Russia.

- Grasslands are one of the world's numerous land-based "biomes," areas of similar climate, animal life, and plant life. Although they can be grouped in different ways, the other biomes are generally considered to be deserts, forests, and tundras.

Millions of Years Ago

The **bedrock**, landscape, and natural resources of the Interior Plains are the result of three main factors. These factors are inland seas, mountain building, and glaciation.

Inland Seas

The inland seas date back to 545 million years ago. Much of North America, including the area that is now the Interior Plains, was flooded with water, creating shallow seas. For hundreds of millions of years, the seas came and went. Each time, wind and water eroded nearby land. The resulting sand was deposited in the seas, along with mud. These sediments became compressed, turning them into sedimentary rocks, which now lie several kilometres below the surface of the Interior Plains. The seas also became home to miniature plants and tiny animals such as **trilobites**. When these creatures died, they were buried under sediment. Today, their remains make up the region's abundant reserves of oil and gas.

> **66** Much of North America, including the Interior Plains, was flooded with water. **99**

Retreating glaciers deposit sediment and cause the formation of landforms, including hills and lakes.

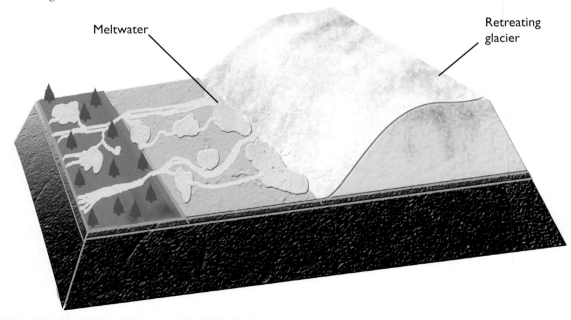

Meltwater

Retreating glacier

Mountain Building

Mountain building also shaped the land, even though the Interior Plains never became mountainous. When Pangaea tore apart, the section that is now North America drifted into another chunk of Earth's crust, causing the Rocky Mountains to rise. Mud and sand washed off the new slope, travelling far across the Interior Plains and adding another layer to its flattened landscape. Most of the sediment was deposited closer to the mountains, so the Interior Plains gradually slopes downward from west to east.

Glaciation

About 1.2 million years ago, a large-scale glacier extended over much of North America, including the Prairie Provinces. When the glaciers retreated, they left a barren landscape of ground-up rock and the occasional deposit of sand, gravel, and boulders. These are today's fertile fields and rolling hills. Some depressions filled with water to create ponds and small lakes. Torrents of meltwater also cut out river valleys.

WHAT CREATURES LIVED IN THE INTERIOR PLAINS?

Over the years, the Interior Plains has been home to many animals. Millions of years ago, the region was even trampled by gigantic dinosaurs, such as the Albertasaurus.

There were also exotic creatures in the Interior Plains, such as saber-toothed cats and llamas. Scientists believe these animals originated in **Eurasia**, crossing into North America over a vast ice bridge during the last Ice Age. These animals included elephant-like woolly mammoths, mastodons, and bison. Other animals, such as camels, did the opposite. They came from the south, moved north, and then **migrated** to Eurasia.

As time went on, the the Interior Plains became drier and warmer. Grasslands covered the prairie area. Perhaps it was because of this climate and vegetation change that as many as fifty species, including mammoths, camels, and mastodons, disappeared from the region within a few thousand years.

Eventually, an abundance of animals prospered in the Interior Plains. Many, such as deer, caribou, black bears, cougars, and bobcats, live in the region today.

Woolly mammoths roamed the northern plains for most of the last 2 million years, until about 9,000 years ago.

The First Inhabitants

The indigenous peoples of Canada were the first people to live on this land. According to the traditional stories of many indigenous peoples, they have lived in North America for as long as anyone can remember. Archaeologists have found evidence of First Nations Peoples on the Interior Plains as far back as 11,000 years ago. This evidence includes remains such as blackened hearths, discarded tools, and cracked bones.

Some groups, such as the Blackfoot Nation, were traditionally **nomadic**, following the great herds of bison that roamed the grasslands in the prairie region. Areas such as the Cypress Hills gave protection from winter winds for both the people and animals. Other groups planted crops along rivers and lived in semi-permanent villages.

First Nations groups on the Prairies include the Assiniboine, the Blackfoot Nation, the Gros Ventre, the Plains Cree, and the Tsuu T'ina. The Blackfoot Nation is comprised of three groups: the Blackfoot, Blood, and Peigan. There are now more than 16,000 people in the Blackfoot Nation.

The people of the boreal plains include the Western Woods Cree and the Beaver. The Beaver traditionally travelled in groups of 25 to 30 people, hunting large game. Before Europeans arrived,

Historically, nomadic First Nations groups lived in dwellings called teepees, which are cone-shaped and are made with buffalo skin and poles.

The Blackfoot Nation obtained horses from Spanish traders.

there were perhaps 1,000 Beaver. Today, there are more than double that number.

The taiga plains are home to such First Nations groups as the Chipewyan, Dogrib, Hare, and Slavey. The traditional way of life for these people was greatly affected by the coming of European explorers and settlers in the last few centuries. Some Chipewyan moved farther south into the boreal plains region when the fur traders made their way from Hudson Bay to Great Slave Lake. Fur-bearing animals were more abundant in this region.

WHO LIVES IN THE INTERIOR PLAINS TODAY?

Today, the First Nations Peoples share this land with all those who moved to the Interior Plains. In the 1800s, many people began arriving in the region from other places, such as Europe.

Often, people moved to the region to take advantage of the rich agricultural land. Today, the Prairies are still known for their fertile soil. Fewer and fewer people are needed to work the land, though, as technology advances. Less than 10 percent of the approximately 4 million people who live on the Prairies work as farmers. Roughly the same percentage live in rural areas. The rest live in cities, particularly the major urban centres of Calgary, Edmonton, Saskatoon, Regina, and Winnipeg.

About 700,000 people live in the boreal plains. Most of them live in smaller communities. About 40 percent live in larger boreal plains centres, including the communities of Wood Buffalo and Grande Prairie.

The population of the taiga plains remains constant at about 22,000 people. More than half are First Nations Peoples. Most of the communities are located along rivers. One of the largest towns is Fort Nelson in British Columbia, which has fewer than 4,000 residents.

Arrivals from Europe

In the late seventeenth century, employees of the Hudson's Bay Company began exploring the Interior Plains. Henry Kelsey may have been the first European to explore the prairie grasslands of Alberta, Saskatchewan, and Manitoba. Following him were other explorers, including Anthony Henday and Samuel Hearne.

66 The success of the fur trade encouraged other explorers to come to Canada. 99

Fur Trade's Big Impact

At about the same time, the fur trade was starting in Canada. Clothiers used the soft underfur of the beaver to make felt for wide-brimmed hats, which were extremely popular in Europe. Soon, explorers were pushing into the Canadian interior in search of more furs. Two rivals, the Hudson's Bay Company and the North West Company, controlled the industry and much of what we now call Canada. The Hudson's Bay Company was granted Rupert's Land by King Charles II of Great Britain. Rupert's Land covered all of Manitoba, nearly all of Saskatchewan, and southern Alberta.

While the main staple of the fur trade was the beaver pelt, other furs, including fox, were also of value to traders.

The employees of these companies helped explore the Interior Plains. In 1690, Henry Kelsey set off from Hudson Bay with First Nations guides. They pushed through the forest until they emerged on the other side—making Kelsey the first European to see present-day Saskatchewan. A few years later, fur traders established posts, opening the Interior Plains to the fur trade business.

In 1870, the Hudson's Bay Company sold Rupert's Land to Canada. By this time, Europeans had changed the face of the Interior Plains and the lives of their inhabitants.

As transportation methods improved, goods were shipped to all parts of the country.

WHO WERE THE HOMESTEADERS?

When Rupert's Land became Canadian property, there were not as many people living in the region as in the rest of Canada. The government wanted to encourage more people to move to the Interior Plains. In 1872, the government introduced the Dominion Lands Act.

The Dominion Lands Act stated that anyone interested in moving to the Prairies would receive land for a registration fee of $10. As long as that person, known as a "homesteader," sowed crops on a portion of the land and built a house, the land would become his or hers after 3 years. When people arrived, they were faced with backbreaking work and hazards such as hail, drought, fire, and swarms of hungry grasshoppers.

Few homesteaders came at first. This changed in 1885 when the Canadian Pacific Railway pushed its way across the nation. Towns grew along the tracks. The railway and land companies advertised across Canada and in Europe for settlers. In 1901, about 400,000 people lived in the Prairies. By 1931, this number had grown to 2.4 million.

Legends from the Plains

BEAVER CREATES THE MACKENZIE RIVER

Legends often tell a story explaining how the natural world was created. The Slavey people have a legend about the origins of the Mackenzie River. It tells how a giant beaver created the Mackenzie River from Great Slave Lake.

A long time ago, in the days before people roamed the land around Great Slave Lake, the lake was much larger than it is today. Back in those days, no river flowed north from Great Slave Lake.

A giant as tall as a pine tree lived at the eastern end of the lake. He was a fearsome hunter with elk skin clothing and a fir tree spear that was tipped with copper from the shores of the lake.

One day, the giant went hunting. He soon came upon the home of a beaver. This was a giant home, large enough for a giant beaver. The beaver was very old.

After much effort, the giant broke down the lodge, scaring away the female beaver and her two cubs.

The giant caught the young beavers and began to chase the mother. The mother swam at great speed through the water, with the giant pursuing her from shore.

When the beaver reached the western end of Great Slave Lake, a huge rock wall stopped her from going farther. The beaver was trapped, and she was worried that the giant would catch her.

In her panic to escape the giant, the beaver smashed through the wall. The water of the lake gushed after her, sweeping the beaver far away from the giant.

This is how the giant beaver created the Mackenzie River from Great Slave Lake.

BISON'S HUMPED SHOULDER

Some legends explain the origin of plants or animals in a region. The bison that used to roam the Interior Plains were very important to the First Nations Peoples who hunted these animals. The Chippewa have a story that explains how the bison got its hump.

In days long past, the bison had no hump. He spent his time racing across the prairies for fun. The foxes would run ahead, warning other animals that the bison was coming.

One day, as the bison was racing across the prairies, he approached the place where little birds lived on the ground. The birds tried to warn the foxes that the bison was heading straight for their nests, but the foxes did not listen. The birds tried to warn the bison that he would surely trample their nests, but the bison did not listen either.

The foxes and the bison inched closer and closer to the nests and the birds tried to warn them again and again, but the bison would not stop. The bison trampled the birds' nests and kept on going. The birds started to cry, but still the bison continued to race across the prairies.

Nanabozho was the mighty ruler of Earth. He saw what had happened, and he felt sorry for the birds. Running ahead, he stopped the bison and foxes. With his stick, he whacked the bison on his shoulders. Afraid another blow would follow, the bison humped up his shoulders.

Then, Nanabozho spoke. "You shall always have a hump on your shoulders, from this day forth," he said. "And you shall always carry your head low for shame."

That is why bison have humped shoulders.

Not Only Flat

Most people consider the landscape of the Interior Plains to be flat. Upon first glance, this may be the case, but the plains are much more than flat land.

Due to the sediments that washed off the Rocky Mountains over millions of years, the land in the Interior Plains slopes to the east. This occurs in three distinct steppes, or plateaus, called the Alberta Plain, the Saskatchewan Plain, and the Manitoba Plain.

Since most of the sediments were deposited close to the mountains, the land in this area has the highest elevation. Geographers call this plateau the Alberta Plain. It is 1,100 metres above sea level.

At its eastern edge, the Alberta Plain blends into the Missouri Coteau, a long ridge of hills that were created when ancient glaciers pushed the land ahead of them. The Missouri Coteau marks the beginning of the Saskatchewan Plain, in which elevations range from 460 to 790 metres above sea level.

The Saskatchewan Plain ends at the Manitoba escarpment. The escarpment is an area of highland that was once the western shoreline of Lake Agassiz, a massive lake that covered much of Manitoba after the glaciers retreated thousands of years ago. The escarpment draws the division between the Saskatchewan Plain and the last plateau, the Manitoba Plain.

The Big Rock near Okotoks, Alberta, was pushed hundreds of kilometres from its home in Jasper National Park by ice age glaciers thousands of years ago.

Wandering Boulders

Ice age glaciers did not completely level the Interior Plains. Although glaciers covered the land, cropping hills and filling in valleys, they also left behind landforms. Some of these are boulders that are out of place. These boulders, which may have originated many kilometres away, are called erratics.

Glaciers also left moraines. These hills may have built up at the side or front edges of a glacier, or side-by-side glaciers may have flattened them into a long ridge. Many moraines created the rolling hills that mark the landscape of the Interior Plains.

Ponds and Lakes

Other moraines have transformed into the region's numerous ponds and lakes. Ponds and lakes have also formed from large blocks of ice that stayed behind when glaciers retreated. When ice blocks melted, they left depressions in the land. Some of these depressions are filled with water year-round, making kettle lakes. Other depressions fill up only when precipitation is high, creating temporary wetlands known as "prairie potholes."

Wetlands also appear for other reasons. In the northern areas of the region, **permafrost** acts as a barrier to water.

Old farmlands may be transformed into wetlands if precipitation drains poorly or does not evaporate efficiently.

Rainfall and snowmelt cannot drain away, and cold temperatures prevent the water from evaporating. The land then becomes soaked in water, developing into bogs called muskeg.

QUICK FACTS

- There are between 1.6 and 7.1 million wetlands in the prairies, depending on precipitation in the area.

- If all of the lakes in the prairie area were gathered in one spot, they would cover 7,800 square kilometres.

- At the mouth of the Mackenzie River, small, cone-shaped islands called "pingos" jut from the water. Pingos are humps of frozen land forced upward by pressure from underground waters.

- "Muskeg" comes from the Algonquian word for "grassy bog."

Unique Landforms

Although much of the land throughout the Interior Plains is uniform, several features stand out. The Mackenzie River, the Cypress Hills, and the badlands in Alberta are unique landforms.

Mackenzie River

The Mackenzie River marks the landscape of the taiga plains. The river flows north from Great Slave Lake to the Beaufort Sea, which opens into the Arctic Ocean. The Mackenzie River travels a distance of over 1,700 kilometres. It is the main stem of a much larger river system and is fed by the Peace, Athabasca, and Liard Rivers. The Mackenzie River and its **tributaries** travel a distance of about 4,250 kilometres and drain an area of 1.8 million square kilometres—larger than the province of Quebec. This means that all the waters flowing through this area find their way into the Mackenzie River and out into the Arctic Ocean. Only three other river systems, all found in Russia, send out this much water into the Arctic Ocean.

> **"** The Mackenzie River is the main stem of a much larger river system and is fed by the Peace, Athabasca, and Liard Rivers. **"**

There are many upland areas offering magnificent views of the various landforms on the Interior Plains.

Cypress Hills

Rising 600 metres above the surrounding Prairies of southern Saskatchewan and Alberta, the Cypress Hills have an elevation of almost 1,500 metres. They form the highest land between the Rocky Mountains and Newfoundland and Labrador. The Cypress Hills are one of the few places in Canada that were high enough to escape being covered in ice during the last Ice Age. Springs that trickle from the hills increase the humidity of the region and allow it to support forests, grasslands, and many types of plants and animals that generally prefer mountainous areas.

Badlands

The badlands of Alberta are another unique landform of the Interior Plains. As glaciers melted, they cut into soft sedimentary rocks. The badlands are steeply sloped and nearly barren. Strangely shaped "hoodoos" dot the landscape. Canada's largest area of badlands extends for about 300 kilometres along the Red Deer River. Part of this area includes Dinosaur Provincial Park, which is a United Nations World Heritage Site.

Hoodoos were carved into fantastic shapes by wind, rain, and water.

QUICK FACTS

- In one place, the Mackenzie River is more than 6 kilometres wide. At another place, steep canyon walls force the river to surge through an opening only 0.5 kilometres wide.

- The Mackenzie River system is the second largest river system in North America. The largest is the Mississippi–Missouri River system in the United States.

- The Cypress Hills do not have any cypress trees. When Captain John Palliser, a surveyor for the British government, drew a map of the area in 1857, he made a mistake. He called the local trees cypress when they are actually jack pine.

- Bird-watchers have sighted more than 230 species of birds in the Cypress Hills.

- The world-famous Royal Tyrrell Museum, which showcases dinosaurs, is located in Drumheller, a town in the Alberta badlands.

- When dinosaurs roamed the land now called the "badlands," the land was covered with a lush, subtropical forest.

Warm Summers, Cold Winters

The West Coast of Canada is known for its wet, warm climate, yet just a bit farther east, the Interior Plains are almost the exact opposite. They are dry and often hot in summer and bitterly cold in winter. The Rocky Mountains cause these varying weather conditions.

Wind from the Rockies

As warm, moist winds blow off the Pacific Ocean, they drop much of their moisture along the coast as rain and snow. The winds also keep the temperatures steady. When they hit the Rocky Mountains, the winds are forced upward over the peaks, cooling as they go. As the air cools, any remaining moisture is squeezed out. When the winds finally descend again into the Interior Plains, they are mostly dry.

> **The winds are forced upward over the peaks, cooling as they go.**

Dry Winds in the Prairies

These westerly winds greatly affect the prairie region. They whip across the prairies, speeding up the evaporation of whatever precipitation there has been, making the climate even drier. Some of the winds are exceptionally warm and dry. These are

Water contained in snow moistens the soil and promotes plant growth during the spring melt.

called "chinook" winds, and occur mainly in southern Alberta. Chinooks can raise temperatures and turn winter into spring-like conditions.

Chinook winds dry out the prairies quickly. Trees have difficulty growing in this climate because of the reduced moisture. Grasses are the dominant vegetation here.

Moisture in the Boreal Plains

Although the boreal plains are also dry, the land does not dry out as quickly as in the prairies. This is because the temperatures are slightly cooler. The moisture in the boreal plains helps support tree life. Here, summers tend to be warm and short, while winters are cool and long.

Snow and Ice in the Taiga Plains

The taiga plains are very dry. Similar to the boreal plains, the cold temperatures mean that the moisture does not evaporate quickly. Winters are extremely cold and long in this area, and the short summers average only 11° Celsius. Snow and ice cover the region for up to 8 months each year.

Chinook winds bring warm temperatures, causing snow and ice to melt rapidly.

QUICK FACTS

▶ "Hailstorm Alley" is a stretch of land in south-central Alberta that experiences the worst hailstorms in North America. Most of the hailstorms occur from May to July, primarily in the afternoon.

▶ One June 3, 1996, Halkirk, Alberta, had a rainfall of almost 175 millimetres in 1 hour. More than half the area's annual average rain occurred in that 1 hour.

Charting the Climate

A region's climate can indicate what it is like to live there. Temperature, snowfall, and even growing seasons are all part of climate.

Information is collected when studying a region's climate. The maps and charts on these pages help describe this information in a visual way.

Average Temperature

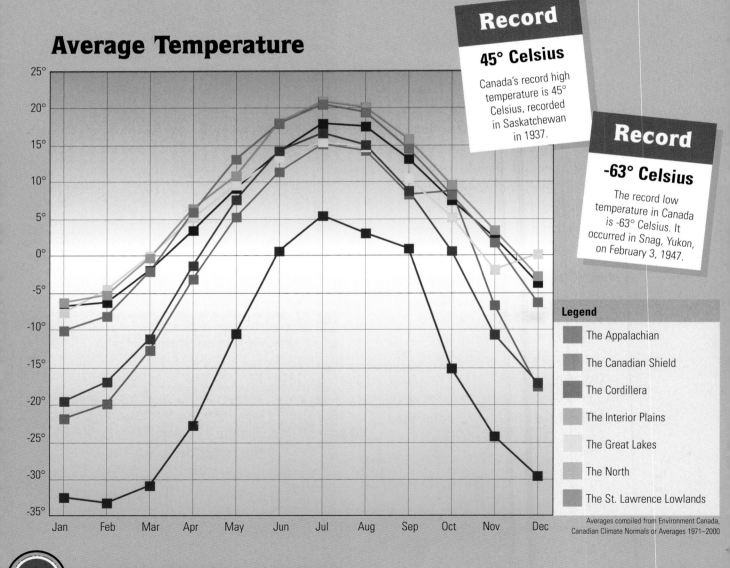

Record

45° Celsius

Canada's record high temperature is 45° Celsius, recorded in Saskatchewan in 1937.

Record

-63° Celsius

The record low temperature in Canada is -63° Celsius. It occurred in Snag, Yukon, on February 3, 1947.

Legend

- The Appalachian
- The Canadian Shield
- The Cordillera
- The Interior Plains
- The Great Lakes
- The North
- The St. Lawrence Lowlands

Averages compiled from Environment Canada,
Canadian Climate Normals or Averages 1971–2000

Average Snowfall

Source: Canadian Oxford World Atlas, 4th Edition, 1998

Legend

- over 400 cm
- 300 - 400 cm
- 200 - 300 cm
- 100 - 200 cm
- under 100 cm

Record

118.1 cm

The record 1-day snowfall, on January 17, 1974, was 118.1 centimetres at Lakelse Lake, British Columbia.

Growing Season

Source: Canadian Oxford World Atlas, 4th Edition, 1998

Legend

Average number of days with a median temperature over 5° C

- under 60
- 60 - 100
- 100 - 140
- 140 - 180
- 180 - 220
- 220 - 260
- over 260

Drought and Depression

There are newspaper accounts and diary entries of droughts in the Interior Plains that date back to the 1800s. Droughts have affected farmers in the region from time to time. They have even plagued the prairies in recent years.

Droughts occur when a region receives much less rain than usual. During these times, the soil dries out and plant growth decreases. Droughts also upset the natural balance, helping to spread certain animal and plant diseases and insect pests. If parts of the land have been converted to farmland or ranchland, the situation may get even worse. If the native plants have been removed or if cattle have stirred up the dry soil, much of the soil may blow away with the wind.

> **" There was little rain in the Interior Plains between 1929 and the summer of 1937. "**

The worst drought in recent history occurred in the 1930s. There was little rain in the Interior Plains between 1929 and the summer of 1937. Natural grasses died, as did farmers' crops. The soil dried out, and the wind blew it away in huge clouds of dust.

During the drought, strong winds blew across the dry land, gathering up topsoil and depositing dirt everywhere.

The Depression and the Wheat

At the same time, two other crises hit Canada's prairie farmers. The first was the Great Depression, a time of severe economic woes. It began at the end of 1929, when the United States' stock m̶a̶r̶k̶e̶t̶ ̶c̶rashed, and continued until the b̶e̶g̶i̶n̶n̶i̶n̶g̶ ̶o̶f̶ ̶World War II in 1939. The s̶e̶c̶o̶n̶d̶ ̶w̶a̶s̶ ̶f̶a̶l̶l̶i̶n̶g̶ ̶w̶heat prices. In 1928, C̶a̶n̶a̶d̶a̶'̶s̶ ̶f̶a̶r̶m̶e̶r̶s̶ ̶h̶a̶d̶ ̶produced so m̶u̶c̶h̶ ̶w̶h̶e̶a̶t̶ ̶t̶h̶a̶t̶ ̶p̶r̶i̶c̶e̶s̶ ̶f̶e̶l̶l̶ from $1.61 a b̶u̶s̶h̶e̶l̶ ̶i̶n̶ ̶1̶9̶29 to just $ .38 in 1932.

A̶c̶c̶o̶r̶d̶i̶n̶g̶ ̶t̶o̶ ̶t̶h̶e̶ ̶1̶9̶31 census, w̶h̶e̶a̶t̶ ̶p̶r̶o̶d̶u̶c̶t̶i̶o̶n̶ ̶i̶n̶ ̶1̶930 had b̶e̶e̶n̶ ̶a̶b̶u̶n̶d̶a̶n̶t̶.̶ ̶Between t̶h̶i̶s̶ ̶t̶i̶m̶e̶ ̶a̶n̶d̶ ̶t̶h̶e̶ ̶p̶eak in 1932, t̶h̶e̶ ̶t̶h̶r̶e̶e̶ ̶p̶r̶a̶i̶r̶i̶e̶ ̶provinces

HOW DO FARMERS CONSERVE THE SOIL?

In nature, it may take 3,000 to 12,000 years for a productive layer of topsoil to develop. Ineffective farming practices can ruin this layer in a matter of years during a devastating drought.

During the drought of the 1930s, the federal government helped farmers cope with the drought and conserve their land. They helped farmers find new ways to store and use water, or they moved them to areas more suited to their crops. The government provided trees free of charge, so farmers could plant them in rows that would slow the winds, stop soil from drifting, and trap snow. Farmers invented new **tillage** machines, too. These machines disturbed the soil as little as possible.

Government organizations promoted other ways of farming, as well. These methods included rotating crops to improve the health of the soil, adding organic and inorganic matter such as manure and limestone, and allowing ranchlands to rest after cattle had grazed them. High-density, year-round crops helped minimize erosion, as did protecting natural vegetation along the banks of rivers and streams.

According to a 1991 census, 42 percent of Canadian farmers said they help conserve the soil by using at least one method of conservation.

Natural Resources

The Interior Plains are best known for agriculture and for oil and gas. With its rich, fertile soil, the prairie area is the domain of the agricultural industry. Almost 80 percent of Canada's farmland lies in the Prairie Provinces. Saskatchewan farmers alone grow half of Canada's wheat, while those in Alberta and Manitoba grow most of the remainder. Other crops include canola, barley, and oats. In the driest areas, land not suitable for crops is used to graze cattle. Most of Canada's beef cattle are raised in Alberta. Farmers also raise other livestock, such as dairy cattle, hogs, and poultry.

> **"** Oil and gas were discovered in the region in the late 1940s. **"**

Oil, Gas, and Minerals

Oil and gas were discovered in the region in the late 1940s. In 1947, Imperial Oil first found oil in the Alberta town of Leduc, just south of Edmonton. At about the same time, the first pipeline to export natural gas from the region was built. Alberta has since become Canada's leading producer of oil and gas. Some oil and gas are also found in Saskatchewan, but it is potash that sets this province apart. Saskatchewan's potash deposits are the largest in the world, making the province one of the world's leading manufacturers of potash-based fertilizers. Saskatchewan is also a major source of uranium.

Nodding donkeys, also known as horsehead pumps, are used to pump oil out of the ground.

Forestry Farther North

Forestry is the primary industry in the northern part of the region. Timber covers more than 80 percent of the boreal plains. Fisheries are also important in the area.

The taiga plains are even more remote and untouched. Although there is some oil and gas exploration, transporting products to more populated areas is expensive. The region's economy relies on forestry and mining. Most of the landscape remains unspoiled by humans.

The forestry industry is of major social and economic importance to Canadians. It includes logging companies, pulp and paper mills, and sawmills.

WHAT ARE THE OIL SANDS?

Hundreds of years ago, the First Nations of the Interior Plains found oil in the sands along the banks of the Athabasca River. They used oil to waterproof their canoes. In 1967, the Great Canadian Oil Sands company began extracting it for commercial use. A larger site was developed by Syncrude Canada in 1978. In 1998, Syncrude shipped its billionth barrel of oil.

The oil sands are a mixture of water, sand, clay, and molasses-like oil called bitumen. When the oil sands are close to the surface, they are dug up and mixed with hot water. This separates the bitumen from the sand. Much of the water can be reused, while the sand is returned to its original site. If the oil sands are deep underground, the workers inject steam through wells. This heats the bitumen so that it rises to the surface. Once the bitumen is separated, it can be processed into oil and used by refineries to make products such as gasoline and diesel fuels.

Soils Rich and Poor

The Interior Plains contain some of the best farming soil in the world. A mixture of sediment washed down from the slopes of the Rocky Mountains over millions of years. This sediment combined with sand, **silt**, clay, and glacier rubble to create a layer of topsoil that is packed with nutrients. There is also more topsoil per hectare in this region than in other areas. Tall-grass prairie has just over 100 tonnes of topsoil per hectare. Forested regions generally have 8 to 20 tonnes per hectare.

> **"** There is more topsoil per hectare in this region than in other areas. **"**

Organic matter is another important factor in the prairie soil. Organic matter is the decomposed remains of dead plant material that becomes part of the soil. There is generally more organic matter in prairie areas than other areas because prairie plants have greater mass than other plants and leave more material when they die.

Sixty-two percent of Canada's farmland is found in the Prairie Provinces.

Soil and the Tall-Grass

Tall-grass grows in the wetter, eastern portion of the prairie area. It has the best soils because of the **fibrous** roots of the grasses that grow here. Farmers consider these black soils among the world's best for growing. Short-grass occurs in the western portion of the area, within the shadows of the Rocky Mountains. Unlike tall-grass, it has smaller plants that add less to the soil when they decay. Therefore, this part of the prairie area has the shallowest and most nutrient-poor soils.

In the colder boreal and taiga plains, decay is slow. Dead matter remains in a layer on top of the soil rather than breaking down and adding to it. These areas also have thin, nutrient-poor soils.

Permafrost

In areas with permafrost, the top layer of soil may melt, creating a layer called the active layer. Here, plants can spread their roots, but the frozen ground beneath them limits their growth. The yearly freezing and thawing of this layer can damage the roots and create lumpy ground with poor growing conditions. It can also create large expanses of muskeg.

Early frost and snow in the Interior Plains has been known to delay harvest and decrease crop quality.

QUICK FACTS

▶ At Great Slave Lake, geologists have found some of the oldest rocks ever seen. They are more than 2 billion years old.

▶ To be considered permafrost, the rock or soil of an area must remain colder than 0° Celsius for more than 2 years. In reality, some permafrost has been continuously frozen for thousands of years.

▶ A layer of dead leaves on a boreal forest floor can take up to 10 years to decompose because of the colder weather. In a warm, tropical area, this would happen up to 60 times faster.

Grasslands and More

The vegetation of the Interior Plains ranges from the prairie grasslands to the transitional forest of the aspen **parkland** and from the boreal plains' coniferous forests to the stunted forests of the taiga plains.

Three Types of Grasslands

The prairies can be divided into three types of grasslands. The short-grass prairies are home to ankle-high grasses such as blue grama and buffalo grass. June grass and western wheatgrass are just two of the grasses found on the mixed-grass prairies. The tall-grass prairies feature grasses such as big bluestem and switchgrass. All of these grasses are well suited to the region's harsh climate. The secret is their deep roots. A single grass can have up to 5 kilometres of roots and root hairs. The roots and root hairs allow the grasses to remain firmly attached to the ground when grazers, such as cattle, tug on the grass as they eat.

> **" Tall-grasses are well suited to the region's harsh climate. The secret is their deep roots. "**

Short-awned porcupine grass and western wheatgrass prevail in the mixed-prairie grasslands.

In drier areas, grasses mingle with desert-like species, such as the prickly pear cactus. Wildflowers bloom throughout the area, while trees and shrubs flourish alongside rivers and streams, on upper elevations, and along the region's easternmost boundary.

Fescue grasses and groves of trembling aspen and balsam poplar dominate the aspen parkland. Here, the prairie area merges with the boreal plains area. **Deciduous** forests give way to coniferous forests of white spruce and jack pine. Black spruce, balsam fir, and tamarack are abundant. Smaller herbs, lichens, mosses, and mushrooms also thrive.

Plants in the Taiga

The tree species in the taiga are similar to those on the prairies and can grow to be just as large in areas bordering rivers. Generally, trees diminish in both number and size farther north. They may also tilt in frozen ground. Smaller plants and shrubs soon take over the land. These include Labrador tea, leatherleaf, fire snag, and wild rose, as well as plants with berries such as cranberries, blueberries, and currants. Mosses and lichens carpet the ground in the taiga plains.

HOW DO CONIFERS SURVIVE THE WINTER?

The coniferous trees of the boreal and taiga plains must cope with long winters. This presents several challenges. First is the short growing season. To cope with this, coniferous trees lose their needles gradually, keeping them for up to 15 years. This allows them to begin **photosynthesis** as early as possible each spring. The cold weather also makes absorbing water difficult for the trees. Instead, coniferous trees focus on preventing the loss of water through evaporation. As an **adaptation**, their needles are long, thin, and waxy. The waxy needles, along with the trees' downward-drooping branches and cone shape, help the trees shed snow and ice to prevent buildup, which could break the branches. Furthermore, the trees go through a yearly process called hardening. This change makes the trees' tissues more resistant to freezing, allowing the trees to survive temperatures as low as -40° Celsius.

Animals in Abundance

Animals abound throughout the Interior Plains. The region's wetlands provide homes for a variety of creatures and allow animals to escape forest fires. River valleys provide food and shelter from harsh winter winds. The region's animals include large **carnivores**, such as black bears, wolves, and lynx.

> ❝ Canada's free-roaming bison were almost hunted to extinction by 1900. ❞

Many Moose and Vanishing Bison

Large **herbivores** in the region include mule deer, whitetail deer, elk, moose, and pronghorn antelope. Woodland caribou live in the boreal and taiga plains areas, while caribou migrate from the tundra to the far northwest corner of the taiga plains each winter.

Bison used to dominate the prairies. While plains bison still survive on wildlife reserves, Canada's free-roaming bison were almost hunted to extinction by 1900. Recently, they were reintroduced to the Old Man on His Back Prairie Heritage and Conservation Area in Saskatchewan. Wood bison—North America's largest land-living animal—are also rare. Both the plains and wood bison are threatened species. They may one day face extinction if no action is taken to save them.

Pronghorn antelopes are a protected species in Canada. They have been reintroduced to the wild in southwestern Saskatchewan and southeastern Alberta.

Smaller animals in this region include coyotes, river otters, badgers, muskrats, beavers, and red foxes. The black-tailed prairie dog lives in large communities located throughout the prairies. These communities are winding networks of underground burrows that provide separate rooms to sleep and eat.

Life in the Wetlands

The Interior Plains' many wetlands are crucial to various species of waterfowl. Thousands of swans, ducks, and geese use the wetlands as breeding and nesting grounds or as pit stops on long migrations. More than half of all the ducks in North America are born in the prairie wetlands. One species of waterfowl, the whooping crane, is endangered. Its only known nesting site is located in Wood Buffalo National Park, near the Alberta–North West Territories border.

The whooping crane is the tallest North American bird, standing almost 1.5 metres high.

HOW HAVE ANIMALS ADAPTED TO THE INTERIOR PLAINS?

To survive the long, cold winter, animals of the Interior Plains have developed unique adaptations. Some migrate to warmer areas. Others hibernate for the winter. During hibernation, these animals curl up in a warm place, their body functions slow down, and their body temperatures lower to almost the freezing point. Contrary to popular belief, bears do not actually hibernate. They just sleep for much of the winter. Smaller animals may tunnel into the snow, which acts as insulation against below-freezing temperatures. Those animals that stay out in the cold have other coping mechanisms. Many, such as elk, grow thick, warm winter coats. Snowshoe hares walk over the snow with ease by spreading their toes apart like snowshoes. A ptarmigan's feathery feet do the same. Moose sink into the snow, but use their long legs like stilts to walk through it.

An Altered Landscape

I n the remote north, the taiga plains remain largely in their natural state. The boreal plains and prairies face environmental damage because of the actions of humans.

The Effect of Forestry

In the boreal plains, forestry is the main concern. Between 1951 and 1991, the amount of forest logged increased by 82 percent. As a result, **ecosystems** have been fragmented, and many animals have lost their homes. Wildlife is also affected when rivers are dammed for **hydroelectricity**. Dams block the flow of the river, meaning fish, such as salmon, can no longer migrate. Fish populations also suffer because of increased fishing and pollution from sources such as farms and acid rain.

Alberta's Oldman River Dam supplies irrigation to many farms in southern Alberta.

The Effect of Agriculture

The most serious threat facing the Interior Plains is agriculture. Nearly 95 percent of the prairies have been converted to farmland. Only 5 percent of its natural state, such as the areas that are too hilly or too dry to farm, are intact. Of the tall-grass grasslands, less than 1 percent remains. Only 18 percent of the short-grass prairie remains, and of the fescue grass prairie, only 24 percent. These statistics make the prairie area the most altered of all of Canada's regions. It is also one of the most endangered. About 70 percent of the wetlands that used to mark the landscape have been destroyed. Many of the area's animals have diminished in population and range because crops have replaced their food sources.

Q	Selective cutting is the process by which a certain type or size of tree is removed from an area. Should this be the method of choice for loggers?	
	NO	**YES**
	Wood harvested through selective cutting is more expensive. It requires the use of sophisticated machinery and a skilled work force. Harvesting also takes longer with selective cutting.	Selective cutting is not as destructive to the ecosystem. Animal **habitat** is less affected.
	Loggers who work around still-standing trees face more safety risks than those who do not.	The remaining trees hold the soil in place, reducing erosion.
	As fewer trees are taken from a given area, more areas must be logged. This means additional forestry roads cut through the landscape.	New growth can occur naturally, without the expense of tree planters.

View from Above

There are different ways to view a region. Maps and photos, including those from satellites, help to show the region in different ways.

A map is a diagram that shows an area's surface. Maps can demonstrate many details, such as lakes, rivers, borders, towns, and even roads.

Photos can demonstrate what a region looks like close up. In a photo, specific objects, such as buildings, people, and animals, can be seen.

Satellite photos are pictures taken from space. A satellite thousands of metres in the air can show details as small as a car.

Questions:

What information can be obtained from a photo?

How might a map be useful?

What details are indicated on a satellite photo that cannot be seen on a map?

McGregor Lake

Lake Neveil

Forest fire

Rocky Mountains

Alberta

Montana

Satellite Image of Interior Plains

Forest and prairie fires are common in the dry Interior Plains during hot summer months. The raging fires send up plumes of thick grey smoke that can be seen from outer space. Although destructive, such fires can actually be helpful for the prairies. Fire releases the nutrients locked in vegetation, enriching the soil. It also clears the land of litter and debris, creating more space for new plants to grow and making grazing easier for cattle and bison.

What do you notice about this satellite photo compared to a regular photo? What information can you learn from it that you would not learn from a map?

Technology Tools

People have studied geology for hundreds of years. Geologists study the rocks, earth, and surfaces that make up Earth. Even before the science of geology had a name, ancient peoples studied the rocks and minerals around them. They experimented to find out what kind of rocks were used to make weapons, jewellery, and items they needed in daily life. Flint, a type of rock that is easy to shape and sharpen, was used to make spears. Minerals, such as gold and copper, were too soft to use as weapons or tools and were shaped to make beautiful jewellery.

Today, geologists use some tools that have been around for centuries, as well as more modern tools. These tools range from simple pick hammers to sophisticated computer equipment. Geologists use these tools to study the rocks and minerals they find on land. They study geology in other areas, as well. Modern technology and tools help them study geology under the sea, in volcanoes, and even on the Moon.

Careers in Geology

What is an environmental geologist?

Answer: Environmental geologists study the issues that arise from the relationships between humans and the natural environment. They focus on societal needs such as access to water, protection of water sources, waste disposal, and natural hazards. Environmental geologists work in a number of areas, including environmental law, environmental education, land-use planning, water supply development, and hydrogeology.

Tools of the Trade

Rock hammer or pick: These special hammers have a flat end that is used to crush larger pieces of rock, and a pointed end, which is used to pick away smaller pieces of rock.

X rays: X rays help geologists study material in detail. Certain crystals or minerals can be examined very closely by an X ray. Geologists studying ancient fossils or artifacts also use X rays so they can examine delicate objects without damaging them.

Compass: A compass helps geologists tell which direction they are going. Compasses are very important to geologists, who often work from maps to travel to the areas they are studying.

Seismograph: A seismograph measures Earth's vibrations. Geologists use seismographs to study the movements of Earth's tectonic plates. Tectonic plates are huge slabs of rock that shift and move beneath Earth's surface. When two or more plates collide, there is an earthquake.

Brushes: Some of the rocks and materials geologists study are very delicate. Once geologists have uncovered an object in the rock or soil, they use soft brushes to remove dust and debris without causing damage.

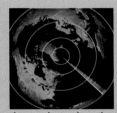

Sonar: Sonar helps geologists map areas that cannot be reached by humans or seen by the human eye. Sonar sends out a beam of sound. Geologists determine what the sonar has hit by the type of vibration that returns. They can map these locations by listening to the sound.

What is a cartographer?

Answer: Cartographers are people who make maps and charts. They take raw data and present it graphically so that it makes sense on paper. Cartography is a rewarding career for people who have good design skills, as well as a strong understanding of physical geography.

Map a Settlement

Before the homesteaders arrived in the Interior Plains, the federal government had to decide exactly where they would go. This involved mapping the region, determining where each lot would be, then staking the ground. Developers today perform the same steps. Here is how you can create your own settlement, too.

1. Use your imagination to come up with an area you would like to develop.

2. Draw the outline of the area. Then sketch in any major features that already exist, such as streams, hills, or roads.

3. Divide the area into individual farmers' lots. In large, empty spaces, you can do what they did on the prairies. Simply determine the boundaries by drawing a grid of horizontal and vertical lines. In areas where you drew large natural features, you may have to be more creative. Leave room for any other features you would like in your settlement, such as playgrounds or stores.

4. Pick your favourite lot and claim it as your own. Imagine where you would build your home and what kinds of crops you would sow.

Sedimentary Education

The bedrock of the Interior Plains started forming millions of years ago when sediments dropped to the bottom of the region's inland seas. In this experiment, you will see how this happens.

Materials

Clear plastic pop bottle with the top cut off, or clear glass jug
Small stones, sand, and soil
Water
Long spoon

1. Throw a handful each of stones, sand, and soil into the bottle. Fill the bottle with water. Stir the contents thoroughly. Let the bottle sit.

2. The contents will eventually settle. When they have, look at the bottle from the side. You can now see how the items you added have settled in distinct layers. Bits of dead plant matter from the soil may float on the top. The water will be in the middle. On the bottom, the heaviest particles will have settled. If these heaviest particles, called sediment, were to be compressed over time, they would become sedimentary rock—just like the bedrock of the Interior Plains.

Further Research

Books

Find out more about Canada's regions and landscapes.

Kaplan, Elizabeth. *Biomes of the World: Taiga*. New York: Benchmark Books, 1996.

Sayre, April Pulley. *Exploring Earth's Biomes: Grassland*. New York: Twenty-First Century Books, 1994.

Web Sites

To learn more about the Interior Plains region, visit:

The Canadian Encyclopedia—Interior Plain
http://www.thecanadianencyclopedia.com/

To learn more about the prairies, the boreal plains, and the taiga plains, visit:

Canadian Biodiversity—Canada's Ecozones
www.canadianbiodiversity.mcgill.ca/english/ecozones/index.htm

Glossary

adaptation: a change made to fit into a certain environment

bedrock: the solid rock that lies beneath the soil

carnivores: animals that eat other animals

coniferous: a type of tree that has needles, produces cones, and generally keeps its leaves over the winter

deciduous: a type of tree that sheds its leaves each fall

ecosystems: the interaction of all the living things of particular environments with one another and with the place that they live

Eurasia: Europe and Asia

fescue: a type of grass

fibrous: having many strands

glaciers: a huge body of ice that moves under its own weight

habitat: the place where an animal or plant is known to live or grow

herbivores: animals that eat plants

hydroelectricity: electricity that is generated from running water

migrated: when locations were changed periodically based on the seasons

nomadic: to travel from place to place, depending on the seasons

parkland: grassland with scattered clusters of trees and shrubs

permafrost: ground or subsoil that is permanently frozen

photosynthesis: production of food by plants using energy from the Sun

silt: sedimentary material consisting of fine particles of clay and sand

sporadic: occurring occasionally

tillage: the cultivating of land

tributaries: bodies of water that run into a larger body of water

trilobites: extinct marine anthropods of the Paleozoic era

tundra: an area in the Far North that is too cold for trees

veld: open grazing areas of southern Africa

Index